Simple Thinking: Intelligent Fighters

Why Wing Chun Works II

Alan Gibson

SUMMERSDALE

Summersdale Publishers Ltd
46 West Street
Chichester
West Sussex
PO19 1RP
United Kingdom

www.summersdale.com

www.wingchun.org.uk

Printed and bound in Great Britain.

ISBN 1 84024 299 X

Important note

If you have or believe you may have a medical condition the techniques outlined in this book should not be attempted without first consulting your doctor. Some of the techniques in this book require a high level of fitness and suppleness and should not be attempted by someone lacking such fitness. The author and the publishers cannot accept any responsibility for any proceedings or prosecutions brought or instituted against any person or body as a result of the use or misuse of any techniques described in this book or any loss, injury or damage caused thereby.

Dedication

"If you want to develop your Ving Tsun you must keep one formula in mind. Does the idea you wish to develop make it more simple, more direct and more efficient?"

Wong Shun Leung (1935 - 1997)

Without whom

Clive Potter & David Peterson for technical advice, Lee Morrison for modelling and reality training section, photography by Ben Ingoldby (www.stilsaw.com), additional photos by Ross Mathews. Cover design Clive Kent, Dr. Mark Curtis for health section, Matt Jarvis, John McFarlane, Simon Hayes for proofing and advice, Sarah Brothwell for support.

Contents

Foreword 1

I first met Alan Gibson in Hong Kong when we were both attending and presenting at the '1st World Ving Tsun Conference' in November of 1999. Later on, we began to correspond via e-mail and I was made aware of Alan's first book, 'Why Wing Chun Works'. We eventually traded copies of each others work, and I was most impressed with the clarity of Alan's explanation of Wing Chun concepts, structure and application. In short, it was a bloody good read!

Alan has now greatly honoured me by inviting me to write this foreword for the follow-up volume that you now hold in your hands. As with the first volume, 'Why Wing Chun Works II' presents clear and precise information that expands on what was presented in his original work, providing the reader with clear guidelines on how to develop the techniques and concepts of the system. Once again, it is written so as to be easy to read and absorb, with illustrations that accurately demonstrate all the drills and concepts described. I thoroughly recommend this book to all devotees of the Wing Chun system, regardless of lineage or experience, and congratulate

Simple Thinking: Intelligent Fighters

Alan on once again producing a book that makes a worthy addition to any martial arts library.

David Peterson 'Melbourne Chinese Martial Arts Club'

David Peterson is the author of the excellent book
'*Look Beyond the Pointing Finger…*
The Combat Philosophy of Wong Shun Leung'

Foreword 2

I have known Alan for some years now. He has always shown himself to have a very open mind with regards his approach to Ving Tsun. This is reflected in the various Ving Tsun practitioners who have been invited to his school to give seminars. Alan has always been searching for "the truth" for his Ving Tsun and has eagerly listened to and analysed everything the various people have put forward. Alan's Ving Tsun has therefore evolved throughout the years and is still doing so even now, this evolution is reflected in this, his latest book.

I was kindly invited to oversee the photography of this latest book to give advice on stances and positioning when showing techniques. Alan has also showed a great ability to teach with his friendly, open approach and the ability to articulate the concepts of Ving Tsun in a way that is easily understandable by his students.

I first met Alan when I was invited to his school to give a seminar on the Wong Shun Leung method of Ving Tsun. The concepts behind such an approach were readily accepted by

Simple Thinking: Intelligent Fighters

both Alan and his students, as they made good practical sense as a way to express Ving Tsun. Since that time I have had the pleasure of being invited to give seminars at Alan's school a few times every year and recently Alan has expressed a wish that he be recognised as part of the Wong Shun Leung Ving Tsun Kung Fu Association UK.

At times Alan visits the Wong Shun Leung Ving Tsun Kung Fu Association UK in St. Albans bringing with him a group of his students to share training with my already established class. In fact a number of Alan's students are accompanying myself and my students to Hong Kong in November 2002 to visit Wong's schools over there. I hope that anyone reading this book will find it of value to them in their training and I give my best wishes to Alan Gibson whom I see not just as a student but also as a good friend."

Introduction

This book is intended to act as a progression from my first book *Why Wing Chun Works*. That book systematically explains the principles that the Wing Chun system is based around and the drills that are designed to internalise them. In this book I will explain how individual techniques and positions evolve, as a result of the underlying concepts and the forces we are likely to meet in combat. I would advise you to read Why Wing Chun Works first unless you are familiar with the basic principles.

Wing Chun is a simple system based on common sense, directness, practicality and self-development and it will be devastatingly effective if you keep it that way. Paradoxically keeping things simple can be difficult, unless you constantly check back to the basic principles. For this reason I will always refer to the central Wing Chun adages:

1.   Hand comes - detain. Hand goes - follow. Hand free – Hit (only don't hit if you can't). The famous saying in Hong Kong concerning this is "Meet what comes, follow what goes, attack when the hands are free".

Simple Thinking: Intelligent Fighters

2.   Fight the person not the hands.

3.   Do not strike until you are within one step of the enemy.

4.   Attack and defend simultaneously.

5.   Do not meet force with force.

The Wing Chun forms are also important cross-reference points. The forms demonstrate the correct positions and movements, as well as illustrating possible scenarios and broad concepts. Mechanical efficiency and economy of movement are the cornerstones of the Wing Chun system; attention to these details must be paid at all times during training.

In the midst of conflict there is barely time to react appropriately, even if you perform your Wing Chun perfectly. Every time you don't do the most simple, and correct technique, you run the risk of being hit. Every time you get hit, you run the risk of being knocked down or out. It is unrealistic to expect to come away from a fight without being hit, but we must try to minimise the chance of this happening. One of the best ways to do this is to follow the rules of Wing Chun and train for maximum effect, with the minimum of effort.

Sometimes, the simplest actions are easy to miss, and often they are not the most natural or instinctive movements. The stress of a conflict situation will also diminish your ability to reproduce fine motor skills. This is why we use drills like *Chi Sau, Lap sau and Single Sticking Ha*nds to programme in refined responses to attacks that threaten our centre or structure. Sensible application of these training methods and principles will create intelligent fighters, who are able to learn how to fight more efficiently.

Practising Wing Chun purely as an art form will not diminish its effectiveness in confrontation. It is however, necessary to understand and train for, the psychological and physiological responses that the body will produce in these stressful situations.

Whilst actual fighting (pitting one individual against another) is one way of demonstrating how effective a system is, we can also train with other people and talk about our different interpretations. If we look at individual skills and personalities we are probably missing the point. Other people will not be able to fight for you. If we look purely at the *system* in terms of the rules and simplicity, we will be able to determine the real benefits of doing one thing or another. Through exploring different avenues we will find the shortest route and access our art to the highest level.

Learning Wing Chun is not a process of collecting techniques, it is a process of stripping away the unnecessary. This is can be seen as being like a sculptor, chipping away at a rough stone until the true beauty of form is revealed.

Some of the ideas or techniques in this book may be slightly different from your own, or that which you have been taught. However, I learned all my skills from people who were prepared to share ideas with me. Wing Chun tells us to enquire, and attempt to improve our thinking and actions. It is a self-development of concepts and ideas.

Chapter I
Conditioning and ancillary training for Wing Chun

The best form of conditioning for Wing Chun skills will always be regular, correct practice (perfect practice makes perfect), especially with the forms. This is because they are specifically designed to systematically train the correct muscles and habits. Attention to detail is very important here, as the first form Siu Lim Tau tells us; small things matter.

However, there are several other practical exercises you can do which will help condition the body. A sensible warm up and stretching regime (found in any sports manual) is always a good place to start before training. Here are some other training drills that I like to use.

In terms of exercises, traditionally Wing Chun in Hong Kong advocates flexibility in the upper body, especially the shoulders, as well as power training. But, for the lower half, cardiovascular exercises are best such as running, skipping etc., to develop lightness on the feet and mobility (both Bruce Lee and Wong Shun Leung were good dancers!).

Leg Conditioning

Stand in a forward leg stance and get a partner to apply pressure with their hands, just above your lead knee. Step forward pushing powerfully with your rear leg, causing your partner to be forced back across the room. This will train leg and stance power.

Pic 001 *Stance power training*

Conditioning and ancillary training for Wing Chun

The rickshaw. Lift you leg as if kicking. Get a partner to support the leg, at waist height, behind the knee and heel. Your partner should then slowly drag you forward. You will need to hop forward whilst trying to push your foot back down to the ground, (you can chain punch at the same time). When you reach the end of the room, your partner can then push you backwards while you do the same thing. This will train the legs and stance for stability and power.

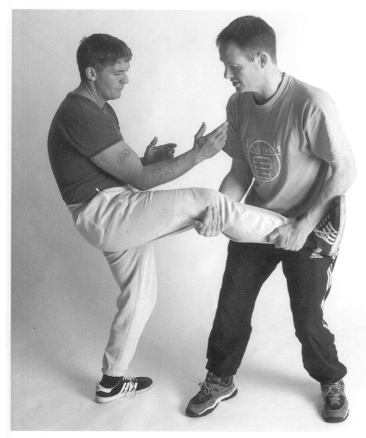

Pic 002 *The rickshaw*

Simple Thinking: Intelligent Fighters

In a forward stance, get a partner to apply pressure, into to a lead or rear hand punch. Hold the punch in position, and pushing with the legs, force your partner back across the room step by step. This will train the whole stance and power chain, enabling you to understand the link between the feet and hands.

Pic 003 *Understanding the links in the power-chain*

Conditioning and ancillary training for Wing Chun

Triangle kicking is a good exercise to train leg speed and stability. Perform a fast front kick, swiftly followed by a downward side-kick, then a stamping kick (across your supporting leg), and then repeat. The kicks should all be fast and controlled, do not put your kicking foot onto the floor. If you feel unbalanced, reverse the order of the kicks and stabilize your stance from the hip.

Pic 004 a-c *Triangle Kicking*

Waist training

From a normal stance rotate slowly at the waist, first to one side, then the other. Gradually increase the speed of the rotation, whilst narrowing the angle and changing the guard arm (or cross punching) each time. If the elbows are held low, you should feel the movement developing in the legs, coming up via the waist and hips and driving the elbows forward. This will train stance and abdominal power, as well as being very good for strength and stability.

Pic 005 *Rapid stance turning trains the whole body*

Conditioning and ancillary training for Wing Chun

In a normal stance hold the arms in a circle in front of you. Relax the torso and bend backwards taking the arm circle with you. Slowly rotate the torso at the waist, from one side to the other. This will develop waist, abdominal and thigh strength. Do not attempt this exercise if you have a bad back!

Pic 006 *Training for waist strength*

Arm training

Form the shapes Bong sau, Tan sau or Fook sau. Keeping the hand and forearm relaxed, move the elbow in a small circle parallel with the floor. After twenty repetitions reverse the direction and repeat. This will train the shoulder and elbow for good mobility and strength.

Pic 007 *Small circle shoulder training*

Conditioning and ancillary training for Wing Chun

Hold a punch out at full stretch. Using your other hand, hold the fist still. Now rotate your elbow till it points downward, then rotate till it points outward, repeat several times. In time you will be able to perform this exercise without holding your fist still with the other hand. This exercise will develop control of the elbow position.

Pics 008 a-b *Controlling elbow position*

Impact training

It is important to train to strike with impact. Punching against a wall bag, or with heavy focus mitts will do this. Performing palm strikes or punching against a wall bag filled with sand or plastic beads, will help to develop penetrative striking power. It will also train the wrists, elbow position, strength, your use of stance and your whole body motion.

Pics 009 a-d *Focus Mitt training*

Simple Thinking: Intelligent Fighters

Practise hitting the bag with different types of blows, from unusual angles and from very close range. This will also teach you how to hit hard without over-committing your body weight. A heavy bag is also very good for linking the hands, waist and stance for powerful impact. Floor to ceiling balls are excellent for hand to eye co-ordination (these can be made simply by tying a tennis ball inside a pair of tights).

Pics 009 e-f Wall bag training

Pics 009 g-h Heavy bag training

The wooden dummy is a great training tool for correct kicking. Kicks should be driven up from the floor, with pressure supplied by the rear leg. In this way any recoil from the dummies springs will be diverted back into your stance, and therefore the floor. If your body bounces back after kicking, you are not kicking correctly. Be sure to kick with the heel, to avoid damaging your ankle and foot ligaments.

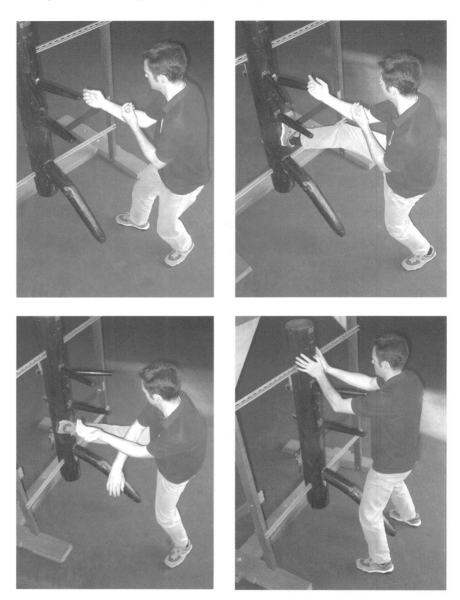

Pics 010 a-d *Impact training on a dummy*

Chapter 2
Getting Started

To achieve a strong attack you will need a good stance. The position for this is given in the opening of the first form (indicating its importance). The feet are about shoulder width apart and turned in. This position makes the feet pronate, making them more stable on the ground.

The knees are bent for stability and mobility. The pelvis is rotated, pushing upwards towards the front, and the buttocks are clenched. This action also pushes the knees outward, positioning them over the feet. It is important to stress that the knees at this point do NOT bend any further. When they are slightly bent at the beginning of the form, they do not bend any further as the feet are positioned for the stance. It is very important to maintain this position as you move about; otherwise your whole posture will be compromised.

The shoulders should be relaxed, or pushed slightly downwards towards the hips. The elbows should be lower than the fists, to allow the shoulder to sit naturally. You should now have a straight line from your knees, through the hips, and to the shoulders. This structure lets the body to turn or step as a strong, unified structure, and this enables us to attack with the power of our whole body, whilst allowing the arms to stay relaxed.

Pic 011 *Correct stance, note the line from the shoulder to the knee*

The simplest attack is a straight punch or palm strike down the centre line (the shortest distance between your hands and your enemy), so this is what we always try to achieve. Any other technique is the result of the simple attack being deflected away from the target, or our own safety being threatened by an incoming attack. Even if our initial attack is deflected, we should still be looking for another simple straight-line attack from the next hand (it is important to position the hand that is not hitting in the correct place to enable this).

The forearms should always point at the opponents centre if they can, with the elbows held low and pointing downwards. This can be likened to pointing a gun at someone. If they move, you only have to pull the trigger. If the gun is pointing away, then you have to aim it first, before pulling the trigger, which will take more time. Pointing the arms also allows the attack to slip through an opponents guard more easily and shows less of the limb to the opponent, making it harder to trap. If your palms point upwards, this looks les threatening and will also tend to sink the elbows.

Pic 012 *Point the elbows at the floor, aim the forearms*

The punching arm must gradually rise as it moves forward and the elbow must be below the wrist or knuckles. At the end of the punch the knuckles push out and slightly up. This is to maintain the line of power down through your stance into the floor, and to disrupt your opponent's stance. If the elbow pops up when you punch (this often happens when people reach through or over a guard), you will end up hitting downwards.

Pic 013 *Do not lift the elbow when hitting*

Simple Thinking: Intelligent Fighters

If you hit downwards you will lose the benefit of your stance and the power gained from it (of course it is still possible to hit powerfully downwards using your weight and gravity, but your body will be committed to the movement). The principle of pressing / hitting slightly upwards in order to gain power from the stance with out over-committing body weight, is shown in the opening of Siu Lim Tao form, and as the feet come together in the third section of Chum Kiu form. If you over-commit your movement in a real fight you may well end up grappling, this is not a good situation, as your enemy may have friends close by who will kick you.

Pic 014 *Correct striking with elbow held low*

Try pushing down against someone with a good stance and they will be able to resist the pressure. If you push up using your legs, they will be moved. This is because the legs are strong enough to hold your own body-weight and another persons' if you were to pick them up. Another analogy is pushing a car along. You wouldn't push down on the boot; you would bring your elbows close to the body and push along using your legs. This is common sense when pushing a car, but often overlooked when practising kung fu.

Pics 015 a *If you push along or down your strength is limited*
b *Use your legs and stance to derive power from the ground*

Simple Thinking: Intelligent Fighters

As the strike is sent out towards the target, the shoulders and arm must be relaxed. If you raise the shoulder first, the movement will be telegraphed. You don't want your opponent to know that you are hitting, until after you have hit them. In the same way, you don't need to tense your fist, just ensure that the joints are correctly lined up. If you tense the fist there is time lost while you un-tense it to move to the next action. The striking should be in a flowing motion. As one fist strikes, the other is already on its way.

You should also take care not to attempt to hit until you are in correct range. In Wing Chun this is elbow-to-elbow. If you attack before you are within one step, you will be tense, over-committed and tend to reach in. If you dive into a lake, don't start swimming until you enter the water!

When your arm is tense as you strike, you will not only slow down the action of the punch, but if you get blocked your posture and centre line will be disrupted. When the arm is deflected away from the target (and the shoulder is relaxed), then the body will not be moved by the block, only the arm. If you have paid attention to the centre line, you other arm will now be able to shoot forward into the gap created by the block, to attack the target.

The arm that hit first should already be returning to the centre line, in order to deal with whatever happens next. Usually, the back-hand is NOT in a Wu Sau, but is on line, ready for the next strike. It is not necessary to perform Bong – Lap sau in this circumstance, unless the defence threatens your centre or structure. Wu sau also tends to make the elbow turn out, keeping the palms of the hands pointing up will make your elbows sink.

Pic 016 *Always be aware of your rear hand position*

Simple Thinking: Intelligent Fighters

This simple but important concept is demonstrated and practised in the first movement of the *Single Sticking Hands* drill. The Tan sau hand rotates, leaving the elbow pointing down to slip forward without clashing (do not meet force with force). As Jum sau is performed in reaction to the movement, the attacking arm is moved off centre. Because the arm is relaxed, the posture is not affected. The striking arm naturally reaches the end of its travel and recoils into a relaxed position ready for Bong sau. If the arm is left extended, then the action of Bong sau will be backward.

Pics 017 a *Stay relaxed during single Sticking Hands*

b. Striking arm remains relaxed when deflected

c. Allowing Bong sau to form properly

Give Me a Lever and I Can Move the World

Of course it is possible to deflect an incoming punch with a punch of your own (simultaneous attack and defence). This skill can be simply trained for by drilling against turning punches. Generally speaking punching against a punch can work three different ways; over the top, up from underneath, and diagonally from the outside. The elbow does the deflecting work, by rising or sinking whilst the punch carries through to strike the target. Each of these three punches can be drilled easily.

Pics 018 a *Deflecting punches exclude the enemy from the centre line, across from above*

b*. Diagonally from the side*

c*. And from underneath*

Simple Thinking: Intelligent Fighters

There are no blocks in Wing Chun, only actions that deflect the incoming force. Wong always referred to Tan Sau, Pak Sau etc. as actions, not blocks. The name in Chinese refers to the action of doing Pak Sau, Bong Sau etc., not its position at the end.

These punching techniques (and many other Wing Chun shapes) work because of the advantage of leverage from various different angles. As the contact is by the elbow, (Your elbow controls the enemy's elbow), a triangle is formed from elbow to shoulder to centreline which will create a strong structure for the tan sau etc. *Note: Apart from the action of Bong Sau, the elbow always points to the floor when striking or deflecting.*

Wing Chun straight line attacks and shapes are very strong down the line, but weak in various other directions. This is why we have to face the point of contact with arm shapes like Tan sau or Biu sau, in order to make them work effectively. Initially, arm shapes such as Bong sau, Tan sau and Fook Sau can be trained and understood with a partner pressing along the line of the limb, this also helps the understanding of the stance.

Pics 019 a Pushing down along Biu sau to test the structural strength

Simple Thinking: Intelligent Fighters

To understand this more clearly, imagine a bicycle wheel held by the axle, but on its side. If you apply pressure to the outside of the tyre, the wheel will rotate and your force is dissipated or spun away from the centre. Individually the spokes in the wheel are weak, and would be easy to bend, but pressing on the rim of the wheel makes them strong. In the same way, a matchstick is simple to snap in your fingers, but if you held it upright against a table, and slammed your hand straight down on to it, the match would most likely go right through your hand.

Once this idea has been internalised, get your partner to push across the shape to demonstrate its weakness. When a shape is weak, your position must change accordingly (do not use strength against strength). A simple example of this would be Tan sau being pushed across the body towards the opposite shoulder. As the force is applied, the body must rotate and Tan sau rolls over into Bong sau, creating strength through leverage advantage. The body is now acting like the bicycle wheel described previously, deflecting incoming force away from your centre. We can then start to learn how the shapes work in Chi sau applications.

You can demonstrate weakness of shapes by getting your partner to hold out a Tan sau and try not to let you move it sideways. Place one finger by the wrist of the Tan sau and you should be able to easily push it to either side.

Pic 019 b *Pressing across Tan sau to show weakness*

Simple Thinking: Intelligent Fighters

Another aspect of leverage is that the further up the arm you move, the greater your leverage from the stance. This is because the nearer your elbow is to the enemies elbow, the more control you have through the triangular structure of the action. Arm contact nearer the hand means more muscles are used to support the force. To put it another way, the closer you fight, the stronger you will be. Again this is common sense in daily life, but we tend to act differently when practising martial arts. If you lift a heavy object, we all know to keep it close to the body, straighten the back and lift with the legs (health and safety at work). The same rule applies to Wing Chun.

To test this, stand in your stance and get a partner to press gently sideways against your wrist. Now try to push back against the force (not too hard or you will pull your shoulder muscles). Your partners leverage is too great; your elbow tends to push out making your efforts futile. Now change and get your partner to push close to your elbow. Holding your elbow in place and pushing from your opposite leg, simply rotate your body towards your partner. They will not be able to resist the force and will be spun away from their previous position of leverage. This principle is shown early in Chum Kiu form as the arms unfold after turning.

Pics 020 a *Pushing by the wrist is futile*

b. *Leverage is greater closer to the elbow*

c. You are able to turn easily and attack

Simple Thinking: Intelligent Fighters

One application of this could be if you have slightly deflected a punch off line with Bong sau, and the attack continues to drive forward your leverage of Bong sau will improve until you are in a far superior position (elbow controlling elbow). If the attacking arm is not relaxed your body will be deflected as well as your arm. This is another reason why you need to stay relaxed when fighting and change your attack as soon as it is taken off line.

Pic 022 a-b *If the attacking arm keeps coming it will be deflected further*

Simple Thinking: Intelligent Fighters

Squaring up

Here is a drill that I use in class to get students to react quickly to an unexpected attack; it trains the natural (negative) flinch reflex into a positive movement.

Confrontation (not sparring) will normally start from a range of about two feet. So, put your hands on your partners' shoulders to judge the distance. This range may feel uncomfortable, but so does confrontation. Keep your hands in front of you, as if talking the situation down, at the same time keeping them lined up to attack.

Your partner can then make an aggressive move; this could be a step inward, a grab, a random punch, or a shove. You need to react by simultaneously staying square as they move, hitting the centre and covering the attacking elbows or shoulders. To ensure that you are relaxed, the attacker can then shove your attack away, step back, or attack again. You will need to flow in order to adjust your position correspondingly.

Pic 022 c *Develop a positive flinch reaction, cover the attack and strike*

Simple Thinking: Intelligent Fighters

An interesting point here is that you will sometimes want to react *before* the aggressor moves. This is because you feel nervous by putting yourself in this threatening situation in the first place. If you hesitate or twitch when you feel like moving, this will trigger the attackers reaction, and your defence will be too slow. For this reason you must attack the moment you feel threatened, even if to you, it seems pre-emptive.

Chapter 3
Simple thinking can be difficult

Simplicity and economy of motion are key factors in good Wing Chun. As humans we tend towards economy quite naturally. If there is a quicker route, we tend to take it if we can. This is why people often walk across the grass in parks, instead of staying on the path. Oddly though, in martial arts people seem to stray from the simple route, perhaps preferring to express themselves in a more flamboyant way, or generating power by using gross movements.

It is easy to get carried away from simple thinking by creating complex or interesting drills that are fun to perform; on the surface they often seem perfectly logical and useful, but you have to constantly question your thinking. *Is it the most simple and direct thing you could do?*

Here is an example that I use in class to illustrate simple thinking.

Simple Thinking: Intelligent Fighters

Starting from a crossed arm position, the attacker initiates a rear Pak sau and punches from the lead hand. The partner defends the punch with Pak sau toward the opposite shoulder. The attackers arm is deflected into Bong sau and using the defenders force he then performs a Lap sau and punch or chop.

Pics 023 a *Pak sau attack*

b *Pak sau defence*

c *Lap sau – Fak sau*

It seems like a good drill and you get to practise several essential elements of the system. On closer inspection however, the Lap sau is not necessary. The attacker could simply punch again after the initial attack is blocked. The hand that made the Pak sau simply carries on going forward (hand free – thrust forward) after it has done its job and seeks out the target. This makes the attack simpler, and thus harder to deal with.

Pic 024 *Continue striking through with the rear hand after Pak sau*

Simple Thinking: Intelligent Fighters

In terms of Wing Chun Theory though, this drill is still flawed. The original Pak sau defence is not the most direct route to finishing the movement. When the punch comes down the line to attack, the defender can simply pivot and punch back. Because the elbow is held low, the incoming attack will be deflected and your punch will reach the target (simultaneous attack and defence). The drill is now simple and direct.

Pic 025 *Do not defend, simply punch back down a new line*

Simple thinking can be difficult

This skill can now be practised in a simple drill. Once this idea has been absorbed, we can diversify the drill to add other elements, which will work off the delivery of a straight, or turning punch. We can now train many of the basic moves, such as: Tan sau and punch, Bong sau, Gong sau and Lap sau in a similar way.

Most of the time the Pak Sau, Tan Sau etc. action are executed once the two opponents have made initial contact and felt the direction of the other's force. Normally before first contact, an attack is defended with another attack, at a different angle if necessary.

It is important to stress though, that whilst you may be practising a specific technique such as Lap sau. The intent should always be to land a clean, straight shot if you can. For this reason drills rely on correct forces being given by both training partners. Otherwise you will either end up practising the wrong response to a force, or the drill will break down because you hit the person who was giving the wrong force. This often happens in the *Single Sticking Hands* drill.

Simple Thinking: Intelligent Fighters

After you have performed Jum sau, your arm should now be pointing at your partner, ready to punch. The punch should be at chest height, pushing forward with the elbow held low. This forces your partner to perform Bong sau to defend his centre. As your punch is deflected by Bong sau it should relax, so as not to disturb your posture. If your punch is either too high, or not strong down the centre because your elbow position is wrong, your partner should not perform Bong sau (because he doesn't need to). He should just punch back. His punch will exclude your punch from the centre and land. This is because in reality he would only execute the Bong Sau if he felt his forward force was losing the line as the opponent was deflecting it.

Pics 026 *Do not perform Bong sau unless you are forced to,*
even in drills (only don't hit if you can't)

Simple Thinking: Intelligent Fighters

Theory of Reduction

The exercise described above demonstrates several points of Wing Chun theory and contains an overall principle of reduction to a simple punch. This kind of drill is designed to train students to think in terms of the fundamental principles of Wing Chun on an abstract level, as well as training in useful reflexes and body habits. Conceptual training drills in this vein are a short-cut to learning intelligent fighting skills.

Other Reduction drills

Moving targets

Start with crossed arms in contact and a forward stance.

A designated person takes the lead, stepping forward a few steps. The partner maintaining elbow position and range, steps back correspondingly. When stepping back, be sure to push off the front leg as you move, otherwise the hip position will shift. If the leading person steps back, the partner steps forward.

Once you are happy following movement forwards and backwards, without the range changing, the leading person can start to move about in a random way, stepping in any direction without a pre-determined pattern, whilst still being followed.

At this point in the drill the following partner may find it necessary to change guards every now and then, in order to hold centre effectively. The leading person can also add guard changes and random forces through the centre, which will need to be dealt with in a relaxed way, such as rolling over to Bong sau and replacing the guard.

As the Lead person gradually increases the speed and directness of movement, you will find the following partner ends up just punching and stepping every time a change is made. The following partner should end up dominating the position of the leading person forcing them to make bad changes on every move.

Pics 027 a-c *Remain square on and dominate the centreline as your partner moves about*

Simple thinking can be difficult

Simple Thinking: Intelligent Fighters

Lap Sau

The same treatment must be given to your Lap sau drill. Firstly, every defensive Bong Sau must be a response to a good attack aimed at the centre of the chest, and likewise the counter attack is a response to the successful defence. If the punch is aimed at the head, we do not necessarily need Bong sau; we can simply punch the attack out of the way.

Secondly, the hand that performs the Lap sau, should be initially trying to go forward to attack the centre, Lap sau is performed (in one movement) because there is an obstacle in the way. When the punching arm is blocked by Bong sau, it should be relaxed. Once again, this means that its deflection will not upset the correct movement and flow of the attack, allowing for further changes afterwards.

Pics 028 a-b *Stay relaxed during Lap sau drill*

Simple Thinking: Intelligent Fighters

Intelligent, strategic punching

Many people seem to believe that Chain Punching is the ultimate, unstoppable attack. However, if you just blithely rattle off a succession of punches against a skilled opponent, they are easily deflected. Punches need to be placed intelligently and as a reaction to what is happening in the conflict.

A good comparison is a sniper who only needs one good well-aimed shot, compared to some one who just sprays the area with a machine gun hoping that one or more bullets will hit the opponent.

Using force sensitivity it is possible to throw fewer punches, but make each one count. One good solid strike is worth 20 bounced off the arms of your enemy. It was said that Wong Shun Leung never needed more than three punches to knock down his enemy. The first punch was not always a punch that counted, but a way of entry whereas the second and third punches are what did the damage.

Simple thinking can be difficult

Students must become aware of what strikes will do damage and which ones do not. Strikes that have some sort of contact with the opponent's arm for control of the opponent are rarely powerful enough to do any damage. They are mainly for control and entry. Strikes that can do damage are those that are FREE. They do not have any contact with the enemy until they hit!

To train for this skill, stand in your stance with your guard held out, get a partner to touch, or push your guard arm in random directions. Every time contact is made, change your guard and replace it with the other one, preferably without your forearms crossing. Your stance and shoulders should not move, even if the arm is shoved roughly across, inward or down.

Next, change the guard arm for a punching arm. Now get your partner to press steadily closer and closer to your centre. Every time your posture feels like it will be disrupted, relax the arm that is under pressure and punch out the other arm down the centre. Take care to quickly realign the arm that has been moved; it will be needed next.

Pics 029 a *The arm is pressed away*

b *Relax and let the arm be moved*

c *In order to find the new punching line*

Simple Thinking: Intelligent Fighters

Your partner can now start to move about, and you must follow, maintaining the same powerful structure and relaxed shoulders to prevent your losing the line. Once this idea has been absorbed, you can practise stepping in to attack and following as your partner retreats, tries to block, or attempts to fight back. Remember, your punches should track the centre wherever it goes, and that to be able to reach with either hand, you have to face your partner.

Pics 030 a-d *Step in to attack with relaxed arms*

Kicking

Like the punch, the Wing Chun kick will normally travel from where the foot is, directly to the target. In a similar way the kick will ideally travel upwards, and into the enemy. If you kick downwards or from a poor stance, your kick may bounce ineffectively off your assailant. Worse still your whole posture may be disrupted (this often happens when people lean back, or transfer their weight to the rear leg before kicking).

If you move your weight back before you kick, your opponent will be able to read your intention and if they are pressing you (as they should), your stance will be uprooted. To prevent leaning back the leg that is left on the ground needs to press forwards, creating an equal and opposite force.

When kicking, you should aim to drive the foot forwards, using the power from your rear leg, as if trying to kick your enemy off the ground. Any recoil will then be sent back into the ground via your stance. This type of kick is shown in the second section of Chum Kiu form. You can practice against a wooden dummy; try to kick directly and powerfully into the trunk, without being bounced back by the recoil.

Pic 031 *Kicking up from the floor*

Simple Thinking: Intelligent Fighters

After performing a kick, your body should drive forwards to put you into punching range. It is a good idea to employ kicking techniques when your fighting range opens up too much or if your enemy retreats or gets knocked back. A step and kick can also be used to close the gap in sparring situations or if a partner disengages from Chi sau. Often an opponent will move their hips back to avoid a kick, this brings their chin nicely into punching range.

Retreat steps

Against a skilled, mobile or powerful opponent it is often not possible to simply pivot and counter attack. Often you will need to retreat in order to regain a good position. The Wing Chun practitioner should never retreat in a straight line. You should always step back at an angle, so as to move out of the line of attack and gain a better angle to counter from. You must also try to ensure that your counter comes from a position of superior strength. If you were running away from someone with a gun, you would zigzag in order to present a more difficult target. The same principle applies here.

Simple thinking can be difficult

A useful drill to practise this skill is retreating with Gong sau. As the attacker steps in to strike, step back at an angle whilst pressing Gong sau towards the opposite shoulder of your opponent. Effectively what happens here is that your fixed elbow position is forced; this should lift / push you stance back in response, leaving you in a strong position to counter-punch from. You can then repeat the attack and retreat from the other side.

Be careful not to step too far out of the line of attack, otherwise your opponent will detect your change and be able to follow you. You only need enough angle to clear a path for your own counter. Your punch must replace (not cross) your Gong sau, which should be lining up to strike again.

Pics 032 a-b *Retreat step with Gong sau and punches*

Of course it is possible to retreat and punch simultaneously, without using a defensive shape first. If you can do this, you should. Punching is better than blocking even when you are retreating.

Chapter 4
Chi sau and the Evolution of Technique

Stepping and pivoting in single sticking hands

To develop tactical movement in response to varied forces we can start by using a mobile version of single sticking hands. This is useful for training footwork skills in combination with force sensitivity:

The person in Tan sau instigates the drill, by stepping in with a straight palm attack, the attack should be powerful enough to make the defender need to step back and retreat using Gong sau. The immovable elbow position is forced, pushing the stance back into an angled retreat step.

From this new position the defender can then step back in and attack with a punch. The initial attacker will now have to defend. If the punch is not powerful enough, or poorly positioned, the defender will be able to use a Shifting Tan sau into a strike. The Tan sau will shift the punch off line and allow the attack to be made.

Simple Thinking: Intelligent Fighters

If the new attack is powerful the Tan sau will collapse into Bong sau and the defender will need to step out of the attacking line to open up a new path for the next hand. The front foot of the defender has now become the rear foot and vice versa. It is important to recognise that these moves depend on pressure, and that the Bong sau is a result of not being able to attack back immediately (Only don't hit if you can't!).

Competition or Cooperation?

Chi sau is Wing Chun's unique, fast track training method. It can be likened to programming the body and mind, to react in an efficient way, when subjected to various threats (diminished response – ability). Through regular practise you will quickly learn the sensitivity to deal with random, aggressive movement. Chi sau is the training method that will give you the skill to fight intelligently, but this does not mean that you should fight during, or with Chi sau all the time.

Often there is the tendency to compete against your partner whilst training. You are after all learning to fight, so why not start practising all the time? At this point we need to remember that we might need our training partner more than once. In order to be given the correct forces, to practise the proper responses, you will need to be cooperative. In all the Wing Chun drills including Chi Sau you will learn more quickly by helping your partner, and them helping you. If you fight each other all the time, you will tend to tense up. If you are tense, your technique will be wrong.

Fighting practise has its place and will condition you to respond while under the added stress and pressure of fear. However, if you compete or fight all the time, your responses will be incorrect, your positioning will be inaccurate (as frequently happens in real fighting) and you will not learn thoroughly. This is because you will never have the time to check whether what you are doing is right or not. You will be too busy trying to hit, or not get hit, to think about what is happening.

It is necessary to experience (in order to understand) fear and aggression, and still be able to go forward, confidant that your training will serve you well. Training under stressful conditions will aid this, it will also help to focus and harness your natural aggression and determination. Once a technique has been learned to a suitable level it must be pressure-tested. Sparring tends to be pretty far removed from the grim reality of fighting, but it is easy with the structured use of scenarios and role-play, to introduce adrenaline into your training equation. The experience this type of training gives will prove invaluable if you end up having to fight for real. You don't need to damage your training partner, but you do need focus and intent, and adding a bit of apprehension to your practice makes for a stronger martial artist.

We are not learning how to fight as such ("the art of fighting without fighting"). We are learning a very efficient way of stopping someone else fighting us! The quickest way of doing this is by knocking them down as quickly as possible (O.K. we are learning how to fight). The best way to achieve this result is by training sensibly to condition the most appropriate responses to random forces and threats. This means that you will have to feed your partner with useful forces to help them understand how to deal with them. This becomes more apparent during Chi sau practice.

In an ideal combat situation, you will not need to use your Chi sau skills. You will just slip through the attack, and punch your assailant directly. However, this is not always a very likely, or realistic scenario. The person attacking you would not have done so if they thought that they would get beaten. Chi sau skills come into their own when your own attack is blocked, jammed or deflected off target. They will also help you to predict, jam and deflect incoming attacks, and maintain correct range as you launch your own strikes.

The basic rolling action

You can practise Chi sau in many different ways; depending on what skill you are trying to develop. The first stage should be learning the basic rolling action using Tan, Bong and Fook sau. To describe the processes that take place here, it is easier to talk about one side of the two bodies involved, you can simply reverse this for your other side.

Tan sau (which must be at ninety degrees to the body) is trying to pry its way forward, inside the opposing Fook sau. A slight forward pressure is being applied down its length from the floor to the elbow (which is trying to get inside or past the line of the Fook sau) towards the centre of your partner. Your hand should be relaxed.

The opposing Fook sau (with the elbow close to the hip and the forearm directed at the opponent's centre) is resting along the forearm of your Tan sau (gaining maximum contact), and prying towards the centre, from the elbow and along the line of the arm. Fook sau is weaker than Tan sau because it is on top - this is why we perform three Fook saus and only one Tan sau at the beginning of Siu Lim Tao. The hand is relaxed. As Tan sau rolls into Bong sau, the hand turns over first (like Fook sau), and then the elbow rolls up. This motion sends your rotating forearm across with the wrist on the centre line, and pressing slightly forwards. Be sure not to over-rotate the shoulder joint, or lift the elbow too high, as this will result in weakness. The hand is relaxed.

The action of rolling into Bong sau will tend to drag the opposing Fook sau's wrist out of alignment with the centre (this is what Bong is meant to do), so the Fook sau position must be adjusted by bringing the elbow towards the centre to maintain its correct alignment. Do not hold your elbows in tight all the time (like when your partner is in Tan sau), or you will not be able to attack. The hand is relaxed.

When Bong sau reaches the limit of its movement, it begins to return to Tan sau. The elbow starts to rotate downwards first (Never Backwards), ending up vertically below the position it was in for Bong sau. Lastly the relaxed hand rolls over.

Pics 033 a *The basic rolling positions for Chi sau*

b *Note the Fook sau elbow position*

It is possible to put a fair bit of energy into this drill to make sure that the shapes are working well with the stance. If you do this too much however, your shoulders will quickly tire out. If you are both accurate with your shapes, you will feel compression as they wedge together, this is when you should change to the next phase of the roll. If one partner has poor shapes or posture they will find themselves tensing up, which will cause the posture to be shaken about or pushed back. The relaxed arms and strong posture should absorb any force; you should not bounce back and forth.

Pics 034 a-b *The basic rolling positions for Chi sau*

Common errors in Rolling Hands

The most common error in rolling hands is being too far away from your partner. Often people keep wrist-to-wrist contact all the time. At this range you cannot hit without reaching in. This will also make you tend to emphasise control with the hands as opposed to the elbows. Using the hands too much will make your forearms tense up, causing over-commitment.

Pics 035 *Do not roll too far out*

Simple Thinking: Intelligent Fighters

We need our (relaxed) hands for hitting so we use elbow position to defend. This is more efficient, more powerful, and allows our arms to stay relaxed. The elbow controls the opponent's elbow [see section on leverage].

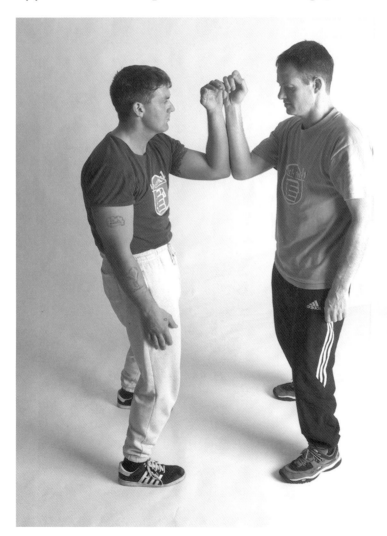

Pics 036 *Measuring the correct fighting distance in Wing Chun*

Chi sau and the Evolution of Technique

If your partner moves out of the correct range in Chi sau, they can also be kicked quite easily.

Pics 037 a-b *If you move out of correct range, you can be easily be kicked*

Simple Thinking: Intelligent Fighters

Other common errors include; letting Tan sau elbow get too close to the body, or holding the Tan sau at the wrong angle. Letting the wrist collapse inwards, on to the centre when performing Bong sau and letting the Fook sau arm be dragged out of position. Any of these errors will lead you into a vulnerable position where you can be hit or forced to defend badly.

Pics 038 a *Tan sau dropping back*

b. Fook sau not lined up

c Poor positioning of Tan sau

Simple Thinking: Intelligent Fighters

If your partner's arms feel heavy, or press heavily on your Bong sau, this is often because their stance is not being used properly. Without a good stance it is impossible to press forward without leaning; this means the body weight is committed. When a partner leans on you, pivot the body to Lan sau (Chum Kiu form, section one). Keep the elbow low but do not bring it too close to the body. This will have the effect of removing the barrier that they are leaning on, allowing them to be dragged forwards onto your incoming palm strike.

Single Stick with Both Hands in Roll

To get used to responding to movement within the roll you can take turns in applying the single sticking hands motions during the roll (the rolling stops during the drilling). Practising using the basic shapes, square on and whilst using both hands is tricky at first, but at least you don't have to think about pivoting as well.

Next you can introduce the pivot on Bong sau, remembering to regain your other hand swiftly for Wu sau, on the centre line (making sure this other hand never loses its focus on the opponent's centre). A common mistake is losing this focus because the pivoting of the body moves the other hand sideways instead of withdrawing it down the same line. If Wu sau is not withdrawn along the centre you can be hit from your opponent's other (Tan sau) arm.

The Four Corners

To learn the basic Chi sau reflexes, you need a partner who can give you appropriate and accurate forces on and around the centre line. To simplify matters it helps to predetermine the direction and timing of an attack, in this way you will be able to train up the correct responses. Initially, you will need to be able to deal with attacks that press to either side of the centre and from the inside and outside gates (inside or outside of your arms). These combinations give you the Four Corners. A slightly off-centre force can be provided to enable a trainee to feel directions of force. Once they are used to this idea, on centre forces can be used. Any attacks that are directly on centre can be dealt with in the same way, depending on your start position and the timing of the attack.

Simple Thinking: Intelligent Fighters

1.   Punching from Fook sau on, or slightly across the centre to the opposite side of your partner's body will create a Bong sau reflex. Note that the other hand withdraws directly into Wu sau. Wu sau then becomes a punch that pins the arm as Bong sau is withdrawn, lining up to strike again.

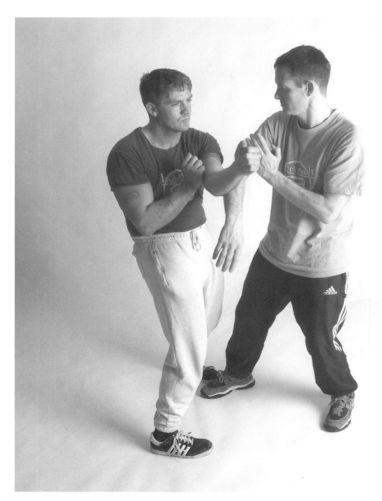

Pics 039 a *Bong sau*

b *Followed by a punch*

Simple Thinking: Intelligent Fighters

2.   Punching from Fook sau, but not crossing the centre line will result in Tan sau to a punch. The body will not need to turn. As Tan Sau is more powerful than Fook, the Tan sau can move directly forward and turn into a strike deflecting the arm, seemingly as one action.

Pics 040 a *Tan sau and punch*

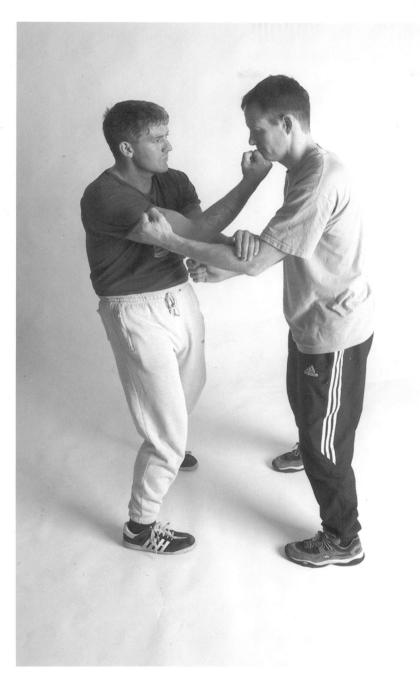

b *Then pin to double up*

Simple Thinking: Intelligent Fighters

3.   Using Gong sau defends punching from Tan sau across, or on the centre. The Gong sau presses forward from the elbow toward the opposite shoulder of your partner. Remember their shoulder is moving as well. Your other hand withdraws to Wu sau and then punches, pinning the arm as the Gong sau is retracted to strike again.

Pics 041 a *Gong sau*

b *Then punch*

4.   Pak sau on the inside gate is used when a strong or fast attack is sent down the inside line, and your Fook Sau arm cannot deal with it. Once the attack gets past a certain point, you cannot stop it without over-use of force. You must abandon your Fook sau, pivot and slip your Tan sau hand across the centre as a Pak sau. Your elbow must move forward towards your partners opposite shoulder to pin your partners other arm, and your Fook sau must return to centre, ready to strike. Do not change your angle when you strike or you will be hit.

Pics 042 a *Inside Pak sau*

b *Then punch, keeping angle*

Simple Thinking: Intelligent Fighters

These four basic moves should of course be drilled in both left and right handed rolling. It is better to learn the roll on your weaker side in the first place as the skill will transfer to your dominant side with very little effort. You will also note that a stepping attack creates a different response to a pivoting attack because of the difference in range, power and positioning. Normally you would step in with the side that the technique is delivered with. This is because, if the top of the body is rotating the same way as the base, you will be more stable and powerfull.

After you are comfortable with these techniques as methods of defence, you can also turn most of them into very effective, stepping motions. These actions can clear both of your opponent's arms with one move, leaving you free to strike with your other hand. The Pak sau technique can also be applied from the Fook sau arm, with the elbow held low and forward to trap the Tan sau elbow.

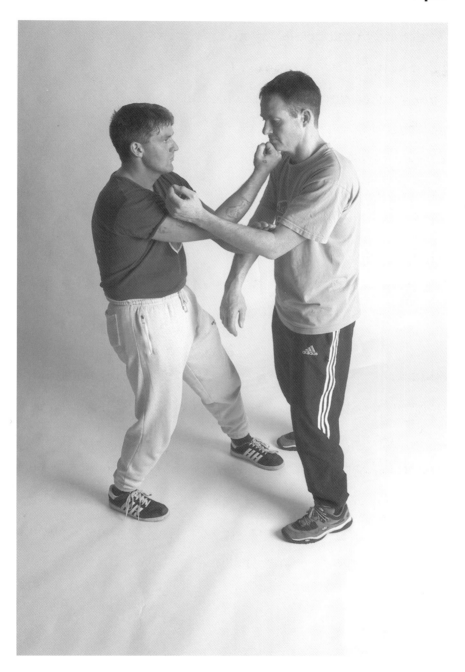

Pics 043 a *Pak sau from Fook sau arm*

Simple Thinking: Intelligent Fighters

To defend this attack Bong sau can be used as a response to the Fook sau's movement. This is because the Pak sau's pinning action moves your relaxed arm into the correct position.

Pics 043 b *Bong sau defence against Pak sau*

Variations on Basic Attack and Defence

It is important to note that this is not just a collection of techniques to run through and practise. The emphasis must be on learning to feel what is happening, not fighting with the forces. Finding the most effective way to deal with the situation through developing sensitivity and correct positioning. We must train the body to react to movement and the mind to understand the principles, in this way we will be better prepared for unusual attacks.

These are not the only drills that can be practised but they give a good foundation. The object is to understand how to control and hit the centre whilst both bodies are in motion and the centre line is changing. Moving targets are harder to hit than stationary ones, so you will need to start slowly and train co-operatively.

The best defence against the Bong sau action is to strike quickly from your own Tan sau arm, before your partner has removed their Fook sau to Wu sau. If they use a stepping attack, you will need to step away at the same time, keeping your Fook sau lined up on centre.

Pics 044 *Hand free thrust forward, before Wu sau is positioned*

An alternative to pulling the Fook sau back to Wu sau when performing Bong sau, is to press it forward pinning your partners Fook sau elbow on the centre or towards the opposite shoulder. This leaves your Bong sau arm free to hit. To defend this attack you will need Biu sau from the third form to free your trapped elbow.

Pics 045 a *Pin the elbow with Fook sau,*

b *Free the pin with Biu sau*

When you step in with Bong sau, the objective is to pin your partners Fook sau across their body.

Pic 046 *Bong sau should trap your partners Fook sau*

Simple Thinking: Intelligent Fighters

To prevent this they can simply step back keeping Fook sau lined up on centre. If you feel them stepping back, you can maintain your forward pressure (lengthening your step by pushing off the rear leg) and drop your Bong sau into a Tan sau, overtaking your partners Fook sau on the inside (like the Shifting Tan sau). This is a good pursuit exercise and is effective against people who step back or retreat a lot.

Pics 047 a *Step back to defeat trap,*

b *Keep moving to overtake retreat*

Simple Thinking: Intelligent Fighters

If you use Tan and punch to counter an attack from the Fook sau arm, your partner can pivot around the punching force and perform a Jut sau technique combined with a punch.

Pic 048 a *Punching attack*

b. Tan and punch defence, *c* Followed by Jut sau and punch

Lap sau and Jut sau

Many people, when performing a lap sau attack from Chi sau, will perform the attack with the elbow out of position. This is simple to defend; as your Tan sau becomes a free hand (because your partner has used their Fook to grab your other arm), it must shoot forward under your Bong sau to strike the centre. You may need to step in to support your Bong sau properly. To defend this attack step back and pull the Bong sau down. Alternatively, if the Bong is too high use Tok sau to jar the arm.

Pic 049 a *Hand free thrust forward when Fak sau is out of position* **b** *Attack centre when Lap sau is attempted*

If your partner's arms cross during the roll, it is also possible to Lap back and down, from your Fook sau onto your partners Fook sau. This move should trap their Bong / Tan arm down simultaneously, allowing you to punch straight down the centre.

To defend this attack you will need to use your emergency Bong sau from the second section of Chum Kiu form. Quan sau can also be used to defend against this attack.

Pic 050 a *Lap down from Chi sau*
b *Defended with emergency Bong sau*

Simple Thinking: Intelligent Fighters

Jut sau (with a punch), seen in the second section of Siu Lim Tao form, can also be used in a similar way to the above Lap sau attack. Remember though, do not move your Jut sau too close to your body or you will bring your partners hand close to your centre. Bong sau with a step can be used to dissolve the Jut sau. If you are late in reacting you can use the emergency Bong sau (as described previously).

Pic 051 a *Jut sau attack*
b *Dissolved by using Bong sau*

Of course I could go on and on and on, adding more possible techniques and attack / defence combinations. In Chi sau, as in fighting, the possibilities are endless. However, as stated before the idea is to try to keep things simple. The more variations we have, the harder it becomes to recall them when they are needed. It is better to try and find a way to deal with many combinations of attacks with a few simple ideas. In this way we will stand a chance in combat.

Training with these few basic ideas will enable you to gain a deeper understanding of the mechanics of Wing Chun, and also how touch sensitivity guides us to the most appropriate manoeuvre.

Technique Evolution

Utilising the skill learned through Chi sau drills, we can start to see how one technique will evolve and flow into another as circumstances change. It is often best to work slowly through a sequence of moves, in order to find the best (most efficient) actions. You can speed things up later, after you have made sure you are taking the best path.

Simple Thinking: Intelligent Fighters

Some examples follow, but remember these patterns are meant to teach a broad concept, as well as being specific examples.

If your partner's Tan sau is poorly positioned, you can attack from your Fook sau arm. To defend this attack you can employ Bong sau or the Shifting Tan sau with a punch, depending on timing and position. To defend this we can employ Bong sau, or possibly an inside Pak sau using the opposite arm.

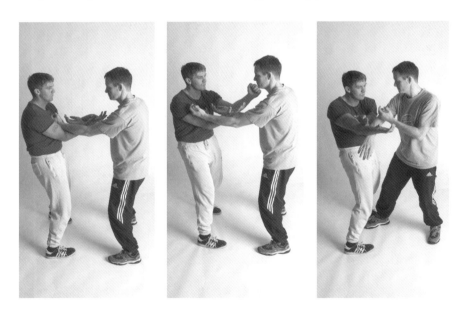

Pics 052 a *Attack over poorly positioned Tan sau*
b *Shifting Tan sau with a punch*
c *Bong sau*

In the same way, if you feel a gap and attack from your Tan sau arm your partner may choose to defend with Gong sau. If they over-commit this defence, your attack should change into Bong sau followed by a punch.

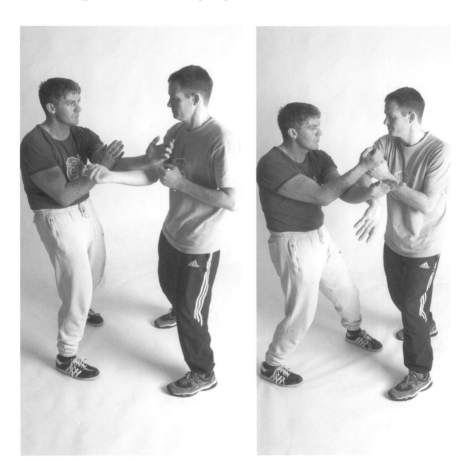

Pics 053 a *Gong sau defence*

b *Bong sau used against over-committed Gong sau and punch*

Simple Thinking: Intelligent Fighters

Quan sau shape will cover both your arms, while leaving one of your opponents' free to hit. To prevent your being hit in this situation, you will need to employ Pak sau from your pinned Fook sau hand, whilst stepping in to press and control the opponents other limb. The simplest reply to this technique would be to use Bong sau against the Pak sau arm.

Pics 054 a *Quan sau* **b.** *Pak sau*

c *Bong sau*

Simple Thinking: Intelligent Fighters

When your Bong sau is pulled down, you can rotate your palm and pin the elbow towards the opposite shoulder (as in Bil Tze section two). If you catch the pin early enough you can use Tan sau punch to prevent this. If you are late or if pushed upwards you will need Biu sau or a punch from under the arm to free the pinning hand.

Pics 055 a *Jut sau* **b**. *Huen sau & pin*

c *Tan sau & punch*

Simple Thinking: Intelligent Fighters

If you have used Bong sau to deflect a punch and another direct punch follows, it is simple to cross directly to the opposite side of the enemy. From this position you could perform a Lap sau, or Tok sau technique supplemented by kicking. Of course, the simplest thing to do would be to re-position and punch back across the line of the second attack.

Pic 066 a *Bong sau defence*

b *Crossing sides using Tok or Lap sau*

c *Perhaps with a kick*

d *Punching is simpler*

Simple Thinking: Intelligent Fighters

If Gong sau is used to cover a lead punch, but the first punch is a feint, you might end up covering the second attack with (wrong) Gong. This leaves you vulnerable to your side. Here you will need to use Huen sau to turn the enemy and line up the jaw.

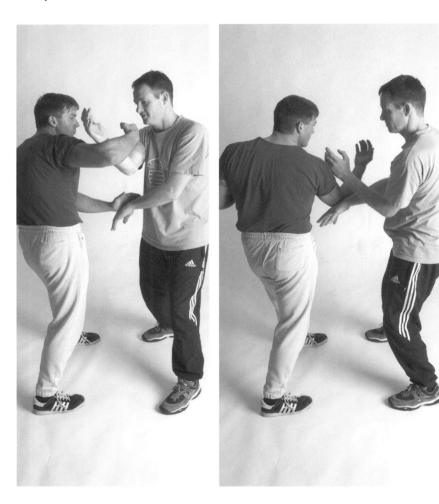

Pics 067 a *Wrong Gong* **b** *Huen sau*

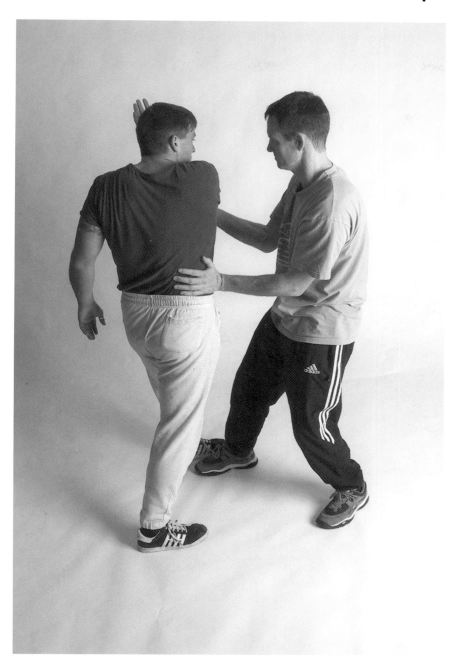

c *pin and strike*

Simple Thinking: Intelligent Fighters

A common error with Huen sau is lifting the elbow as you perform the technique; you will be hit if this happens.

Pics 068 *Do not lift the elbow during Huen sau*

After having used a retreat step with Gong sau (this is also an effective defence against a powerful shove, often used to pre-empt an attack), you are in a good position to move forward again intercepting the next attack. If the second attack is circular, you can move forward, cover the attack with Tan or Biu sau and punch. If your enemy then tries to step around you to strike your floating ribs, you can drop straight into Lower Gong, whilst striking the jaw directly with the hand that is now free.

Pics 069 a *Gong sau against a punch*

b. *Using Gong sau against a shove*

c. *followed by a swinging punch*

d. *Biu sau and strike*

e. *Low strike is covered and countered*

Simple Thinking: Intelligent Fighters

Using combinations of techniques previously discussed, we can see that the possibilities are quite literally endless. Provided both parties follow the rules, there is always an answer to any attack. You will get beaten if you make a mistake though, and we all make mistakes because we are human.

Working through sequential moves in this way, enables you to follow and adjust to a moving target. Starting slowly and analysing as you progress will teach you to flow from one technique to another, utilising correct footwork and body movement. Once you have a good understanding of how the shapes evolve it is good practise to free form. This will teach spontaneity under pressure. You must however, never neglect the basic drills, as this is where your primary skills are derived form.

Chapter 5
Reality training by Lee Morrisson

For us to make the art of Wing Chun or indeed any system accessible in a real situation there are several points we need to be aware of: First we need to know our enemy.

Here we are talking about self-protection against gratuitous violence. This kind of attacker will often enter through dialogue; this can be either deceptive or aggressive, from here the distance will be closed (which incidentally is no more than two feet to start with). Next there will be a violent attack, usually a punch or head-butt designed to knock you down. Once on the ground you will be kicked. The whole episode will last only a few seconds.

Then we have the surprise attack, where you are grabbed from behind or distracted initially. Basically, if you have no awareness, any conflict situation will be an ambush attack, so you need to be switched on to your environment.

Simple Thinking: Intelligent Fighters

Many martial arts schools teach all techniques from a pre-fight posture, emphasising closing the gap to engage in combat. This is training for sparring or a match fight scenario (which requires considerable bottle and honour), but it is often impractical for self-protection on the street.

Firstly the posture needs to be a natural, open handed, non-aggressive guard or fence. The guard should be mobile, use you hands to gesture naturally as you would when talking, but make sure that they are on line and available at all times. Keep the hands up to occupy the space between you and the aggressor. There is no gap to close, he will do that for you. This is why we need the arms - to control the distance between you.

Pic 070 a

From here you will need one or two well practised pre-emptive strikes. Good examples from Wing Chun are Centre punch to the jaw or chest and Biu sau (finger jab) to the eyes. The legality / morality of striking first is complex but it's safe to say it is often the only sensible option if you *feel* threatened and *feel* that violence is unavoidable.

Pic 070 b *finger strike to eyes* **c** *Palm strike to jaw*

d *Push face downward* **e** *To finish*

Simple Thinking: Intelligent Fighters

It is important to train these attacks with impact; the wall bag is an excellent tool for developing penetration in punching, and focus pads should be used to train accuracy and impact. If you practise to strike with impact, then muscle memory will go with the majority if we need to fight.

Finally and perhaps most importantly, we need to address the effects of adrenaline in confrontation. Adrenaline is guaranteed and should be expected, everybody gets this feeling; butterflies in the stomach, shaky legs and hands, tunnel vision etc. If you can control the affects of adrenaline under pressure, you are more likely to be able access your art and function effectively.

The only way to desensitise yourself to these feelings is to recreate them in training through adrenal controlling scenarios. This can be done through Role-play using aggressive posturing, pushing and swearing to the point where we induce feelings of fear but strive to function anyway. When we recreate these scenes the brain cannot tell the difference and will cause adrenaline to flood into our bodies. When you access this adrenal state during training, you will also develop a control over it.

Knowing your enemy, controlling the fighting range, training for impact and being able to understand fear and the adrenal state, will give you much better odds in a real fight situation.

Chapter 6
Health benefits of Wing Chun

Whilst it is vital to maintain Wing Chun's focus, and its reputation as a very sophisticated weapon, I believe is also important to be aware of the other (health and self-developmental) benefits and side-effects you will gain from training in Wing Chun.

Apart from the well-known benefits of strength and cardiovascular training on fitness and well being, Wing Chun will also help maintain a strong and healthy posture. A good posture and an understanding of the body's mechanics will help you throughout your life. Anyone who has experienced back pain, and had to visit a doctor or an osteopath, knows only too well how debilitating this can be.

The basic Wing Chun stance is closely related to positions used in Tai Chi, Qi -Gong and Yoga (as well as some more esoteric tantric sexual practices!), all of which are now recognised as being excellent forms of healthy exercise. If you train the Wing Chun forms on a daily basis, your posture and circulation will be improved, musculature developed and joints loosened and stretched. This will translate into better confidence, general well-being and a healthy life-style.

A Soul Food Diet
By Dr. Mark Curtis

Wing Chun practitioners often comment on how their particular training makes them feel really good. There seems to be an almost addictive nature to it and practitioners often say that it seems to almost infiltrate every part of their life. It seems quite clear that Wing Chun does have certain health benefits. These can be broadly divided into the physical and psychological.

I must start however with a word of caution. Some martial arts try to make the body do almost unnatural things and emphasize actions in their training that can excessively load joints. This is a serious concern. In the long-term this can lead to osteoarthritis (wear and tear arthritis), which can cause much pain and suffering. There is no cure for osteoarthritis and the only real treatments currently are painkillers and joint replacement operations. I would urge all martial artists to

Simple Thinking: Intelligent Fighters

look closely at the pros and cons of their training methods. Even just doing repetitive, powerful, full extensions of the elbow during punch training will eventually damage the joint. There is also the issue of breaking lumps of wood, concrete etc. This always looks fantastic and you can only admire the focus and determination of the individuals who do it, but does this type of training make you any more likely to win a fight, and are you prepared to accept the joint damage that may result?

There will always be much debate as to what are good and bad training methods but in my opinion a true martial art should not be damaging to the body and should be easily practiced into old age. Wing Chun, in contrast to many arts, if practiced correctly, is actually a soft, free flowing style, which deals more with deflecting an opponents energy rather than clashing with it head on. Since the training takes place at close range the elbows mostly remain in a semi flexed position even during striking. These factors help to keep joint loading to a minimum. Minor injuries do occur, as with any contact activity but the system on the whole it is not damaging to the body.

Health benefits of Wing Chun

The Wing Chun forms teach many things including good posture, flexibility, and coordination. The forms have an almost meditative quality and can really help to calm the mind. Chi sau in particular is a fascinating part of the system. It provides an excellent form of gentle controlled aerobic exercise, which improves contact sensitivity and reflexes. There is much emphasis in chi sau in learning to relax and conserving energy and players often find that they perform better if they just switch their mind off. This release from conscious thought can result in the whole training experience being incredibly relaxing and refreshing. I believe that this stress relieving quality is probably the major health benefit of Wing Chun.

The practice of Wing Chun Kung Fu can have profound psychological effects. Most importantly I think, it can provide an enormously positive focus in people's lives. All too often in my work as a GP I see patients who lack such a focus, often they suffer from low self-esteem, depression and anxiety. There does in fact now seem to be some evidence that physical exercise can make you less likely to suffer from depression.

Simple Thinking: Intelligent Fighters

The close range nature of Wing Chun training helps to break down barriers between people and training partners often become trusted friends. In order to learn much of the training is cooperative and it is not necessary to hurt your partner. Chi sau is such a dynamic drill that your perceived advantage can quickly be turned against you. All of these factors help us to realize the importance of controlling our egos.

There is obviously a philosophical side to kung fu, which I believe can subconsciously affect the way you approach life. Many parallels can be drawn between the fighting concepts and strategies and the way we deal with problems in real life. The centreline theory for example could be interpreted as marinating a balance in your life. For myself I often find that keeping things in life simple, direct and efficient works very well. I find that the complexity of modern life can frequently increase stress levels, which puts us at risk of mental and physical ill health. There is much to be said for having a simple life. Wing Chun constantly reminds me of the value of simplicity.

I recently found a wonderfully profound old Taoist saying:" Lessons learnt by the body educate the mind." This for me sums up the whole philosophical side to kung fu but in truth it is up to the individual to discover how it can change his or her life in the course of time.

Kung fu really can be a "soul food".

Contact us

Alan Gibson founded the Wing Chun Federation in 1990. The Federation's objective is to teach Wing Chun Kung Fu in a relaxed and accessible manner, where emphasis is placed on good technique and personal development. Wing Chun can be simply learnt by commitment and patience. Age, sex or physical size is of no consequence, and a high level of proficiency can be obtained quickly and with ease. We are a non-political organisation.

The Wing Chun Federation also runs regular self defence for women courses, where the student will learn the essentials of defending themselves against would be attackers, as well as how to avoid dangerous or uncomfortable confrontations where possible.

Representatives can be found in Southampton, Winchester, Salisbury, Portsmouth, London, Crowthorne, Isle of Wight, and Bournemouth.

To contact the Wing Chun Federation about tuition or to book seminars in your area, please write to:

Contact Us

Alan Gibson

The Wing Chun Federation,

12 Park Rd, Chandlersford, Eastleigh, Hants. SO53 2EU

Telephone: (U.K.) 023 8057 2084

Pager: 07654 220170(4)

e mail: alan@wingchun.org.uk

Or visit our web site at: http://www.wingchun.org.uk

Siu Lim Tao demonstrates the basic reference points in the Wing Chun structure.
Chum Kiu trains us to maintain these points whilst fighting a moving target.
Opening the form, find the stance, find the centreline, and punch down it.

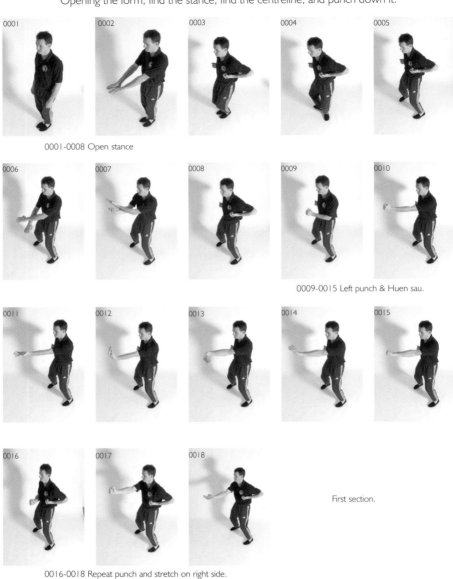

0001-0008 Open stance

0009-0015 Left punch & Huen sau.

First section.

0016-0018 Repeat punch and stretch on right side.

001-002 Double eye gouge   003 Turn to left   004 Turn to right   005 Turn to left

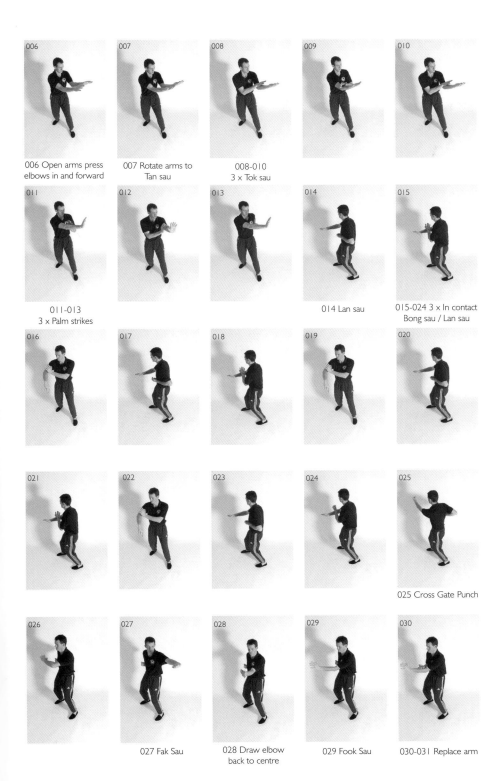

006 Open arms press
elbows in and forward

007 Rotate arms to
Tan sau

008-010
3 x Tok sau

011-013
3 x Palm strikes

014 Lan sau

015-024 3 x In contact
Bong sau / Lan sau

025 Cross Gate Punch

027 Fak Sau

028 Draw elbow
back to centre

029 Fook Sau

030-031 Replace arm

153

032 Huensau

034-062 Repeat on other side

056

057

058

059

060

061

062

Second section

063

064

063 Lan sau

064 Lifting kick

065

066

067

068

069

065-069 3 x Emergency Bong sau

070

071

072

073

070 Punch from Bong
sau

071 Cover and turn

072 Replace arm and
Huen sau

076

077

078

079

080

076-085 Repeat on other side

155

Third section

087 turn

088 Lifting kick

089-093 3 x Double Bong sau

094 Double Jut sau

095 Push without commitment

097 Step back

098-107 Repeat on other side

156

108 Turn and position feet

109 Kick to 135 degrees

110 Step into stance

111-113 3 x Gum sau with turn

114 Punch across gate from low to high

115-123 3 x Punches, Huen sau, close stance

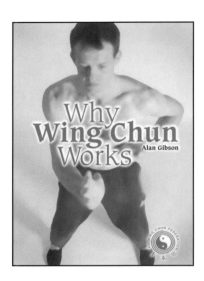

Why Wing Chun Works

The most popular and comprehensive Wing Chun book available in the UK. This in depth study systematically explains all the essential concepts, principles and basic training methods of the Wing Chun System. Why Wing Chun Works is the perfect training aid for anyone thinking about, or already studying, Wing Chun. It will also prove invaluable for other martial artists wishing to broaden their horizons.

Divided neatly into sections to facilitate the learning process and make cross-referencing simple, Why Wing Chun Works covers holistic health and philosophical argument and is clearly illustrated with photographs and diagrams. The book also has Siu Lim Tao, (Wing Chun's first form) completely demonstrated in numbered photographs.

Why Wing Chun Works £12.00
All prices include postage and packaging. Send a cheque / postal order made out for **Alan Gibson** and include your address.

Send to:
**The Wing Chun Federation, 12 Park Rd, Chandlers Ford
Eastleigh. SO53 2EU**

Only available in the U.K. Please allow 28 days for delivery.